קַדִּישׁ

T0265452

How unusual would a love song be if it didn't mention love? Or a movie about surfing that didn't show one surfboard? Surprisingly, the Mourner's קַדִּישׁ, a prayer said in memory of those who have died, doesn't mention death at all. Instead, it praises God, speaks of God's holiness, and expresses our longing for peace on earth. At our saddest moments, we speak words of promise and of hope.

Practice reading the Mourner's Kaddish aloud.

1. יִתְגַּדַּל וְיִתְקַדַּשׁ שְׁמֵהּ רַבָּא

2. בְּעָלְמָא דִּי בְרָא כִרְעוּתֵהּ, וְיַמְלִיךְ מַלְכוּתֵהּ

3. בְּחַיֵּיכוֹן וּבְיוֹמֵיכוֹן וּבְחַיֵּי דְכָל־בֵּית יִשְׂרָאֵל,

4. בַּעֲגָלָא וּבִזְמַן קָרִיב, וְאִמְרוּ אָמֵן.

5. יְהֵא שְׁמֵהּ רַבָּא מְבָרַךְ לְעָלַם וּלְעָלְמֵי עָלְמַיָּא.

6. יִתְבָּרַךְ וְיִשְׁתַּבַּח וְיִתְפָּאַר וְיִתְרוֹמַם וְיִתְנַשֵּׂא

7. וְיִתְהַדָּר וְיִתְעַלֶּה וְיִתְהַלָּל שְׁמֵהּ דְּקֻדְשָׁא, בְּרִיךְ הוּא.

8. לְעֵלָּא מִן כָּל־בִּרְכָתָא וְשִׁירָתָא,

9. תֻּשְׁבְּחָתָא וְנֶחֱמָתָא דַּאֲמִירָן בְּעָלְמָא, וְאִמְרוּ אָמֵן.

10. יְהֵא שְׁלָמָא רַבָּא מִן שְׁמַיָּא

11. וְחַיִּים עָלֵינוּ וְעַל־כָּל־יִשְׂרָאֵל, וְאִמְרוּ אָמֵן.

12. עֹשֶׂה שָׁלוֹם בִּמְרוֹמָיו הוּא יַעֲשֶׂה שָׁלוֹם

13. עָלֵינוּ וְעַל־כָּל־יִשְׂרָאֵל, וְאִמְרוּ אָמֵן.

Judaism teaches us the importance of comforting those who have suffered a loss, for them *and* for us.

May God's name be great and may it be made holy
in the world created according to God's will. May God rule
in our own lives and our own days, and in the life of all the house of Israel,
swiftly and soon, and say, Amen.
May God's great name be blessed forever and ever.
Blessed, praised, glorified, exalted, extolled,
honored, magnified, and adored be the name of the Holy One, blessed is God,
though God is beyond all the blessings, songs,
adorations, and consolations that are spoken in the world, and say, Amen.
May there be great peace from heaven
and life for us and for all Israel, and say, Amen.
May God who makes peace in the heavens, make peace
for us and for all Israel. And say, Amen.

DID YOU KNOW?

Did you notice something different about the language of the קַדִּישׁ? Most of the words in the קַדִּישׁ are Aramaic. Aramaic is a language similar to Hebrew that was spoken by the Jews at the time of Ezra in the fifth century B.C.E. and for about a thousand years thereafter. The last two lines of the קַדִּישׁ are written in Hebrew. Do you recognize them?

THE HEBREW-ARAMAIC CONNECTION

The words in the Kaddish may look difficult but, in fact, you already know many of them!

In the right-hand column are Hebrew prayer words you have already learned. In the left-hand column are related Aramaic words from the Kaddish.

Write the number of the Hebrew word next to its related Aramaic word. *(Hint: Look for related roots.)*

ARAMAIC		HEBREW	
בְּרִיךְ	_____	גַּדְלָה	1.
בְּעָלְמָא	_____	קִדְּשָׁנוּ	2.
וּבְחַיֵּי	_____	הָעוֹלָם	3.
יִתְגַּדַּל	_____	מֶלֶךְ	4.
קַדִּישׁ, וְיִתְקַדַּשׁ	_____	חַיִּים	5.
וְיַמְלִיךְ	_____	בָּרוּךְ	6.
שְׁלָמָא	_____	שָׁלוֹם	7.

PRAYER DICTIONARY

קַדִּישׁ
holy

יִתְגַּדַּל
will be great

וְיִתְקַדַּשׁ
and will be holy

שְׁמֵהּ
God's name

בְּעָלְמָא
in the world

וְיַמְלִיךְ
and will rule

מַלְכוּתֵהּ
God's kingdom

וּבְחַיֵּי

and in the life of

לְעָלַם

forever

וְיִשְׁתַּבַּח

and will be praised

בְּרִיךְ

blessed

בְּרְכָתָא

blessing

שְׁלָמָא

peace

ROOT SEARCH

Write the root for each of the Aramaic words below.

ROOT	ARAMAIC WORD
___ ___ ___	בְּרִיךְ
___ ___ ___	מַלְכוּתֵהּ
___ ___ ___	יִתְגַּדַּל
___ ___ ___	בִּרְכָתָא
___ ___ ___	וְיַמְלִיךְ
___ ___ ___	קַדִּישׁ, וְיִתְקַדַּשׁ
___ ___ ___	שְׁלָמָא

Choose any four roots from above and write the English meaning.

ENGLISH MEANING	ROOT
_____	___ ___ ___
_____	___ ___ ___
_____	___ ___ ___
_____	___ ___ ___

WORD MATCH

Draw a line from the Aramaic word to its English meaning.

forever	קַדִּישׁ
(God's) kingdom	בְּרִיךְ
holy	לְעָלַם
blessed	מַלְכוּתֵהּ
(God's) name	שְׁלָמָא
and will be praised	שְׁמֵהּ
will be great	וְיִשְׁתַּבַּח
peace	יִתְגַּדַּל
and will be holy	בִּרְכָתָא
and will rule	וּבְחַיֵּי
blessing	וְיַמְלִיךְ
and in the life of	וְיִתְקַדַּשׁ

How, in a time of mourning, might paying attention to the grandeur of nature fill us with hope?

5

THE THEME OF THE PRAYER

We have learned that the Mourner's Kaddish is said in memory of someone who has died, yet it contains no mention of death.

Reread the English translation of the Kaddish on page 2. Pay attention to the tone and mood of the prayer. Then do the following exercise.

1. Fill in the blank by choosing the correct word.

   The Kaddish is a prayer of _____ to God. (thanks/praise/request)

2. Choose four words from the English translation of the prayer that illustrate your answer to number 1.

   _____ _____ _____ _____

3. The Kaddish ends on a hopeful, optimistic note.
   It ends with a wish for _____.
   Why do you think the Kaddish ends with this wish?

   _____

4. Why do you think the Kaddish is recited by mourners even though it does not mention death?

   _____

   _____

   _____

1. On page 1, (circle) all the words in the קַדִּישׁ that have the root קדשׁ.

   How many words did you circle? _____

   What does the root קדשׁ mean? _____

2. Put a star⭐ above all the words with the root ברכ.

   How many words did you star? _____

   What does the root ברכ mean? _____

3. Three words in the קַדִּישׁ mean "life." Write them here.

   _____   _____   _____

4. Peace is an important concept in the קַדִּישׁ. Write the Hebrew word

   for "peace." _____

   This word—or a variation—appears three times near the end of the קַדִּישׁ.

   Put a box around each one.

5. We know that כָּל means _____.

   Now underline כָּל or כָל wherever it appears.

   How many underlined words do you have? _____

6. עוֹלָם means "forever" or "world." This word appears five times, in a
   variety of forms, in the קַדִּישׁ.

   Write the five words here.

   _____   _____   _____

   _____   _____

ABOUT THE KADDISH

In this booklet we have learned about the Mourner's קַדִּישׁ. But there are other versions of the קַדִּישׁ, for example the חֲצִי קַדִּישׁ ("half Kaddish"), which is only slightly shorter. The קַדִּישׁ divides up the service, almost the way a file divider separates the subjects in your school binder. It indicates the end of one section of the service and the beginning of the next.

We are not sure who wrote the קַדִּישׁ or when. It probably developed over hundreds of years. We do know that almost 800 years ago the קַדִּישׁ came to be the prayer said by mourners.

In some congregations, only the mourners and those observing *yahrzeit*—the anniversary of a loved one's death—stand as they recite the קַדִּישׁ. In other congregations, everyone stands as a sign of support for the mourners and to remember those who died in the Holocaust.

We say the קַדִּישׁ only in the presence of a מִנְיָן. As the mourners rhythmically chant the prayer, the congregation publicly acknowledges God's greatness. Although the Mourner's קַדִּישׁ is recited in memory of the dead, its words also give strength to the living.

Below are the last two lines of the קַדִּישׁ.

עֹשֶׂה שָׁלוֹם בִּמְרוֹמָיו הוּא יַעֲשֶׂה שָׁלוֹם
עָלֵינוּ וְעַל־כָּל־יִשְׂרָאֵל, וְאִמְרוּ אָמֵן.

May God who makes peace in the heavens, make peace for us and for all Israel. And say, Amen.

עֹשֶׂה שָׁלוֹם is the same sentence that concludes both the עֲמִידָה and בִּרְכַּת הַמָּזוֹן (Grace After Meals). When we say עֹשֶׂה שָׁלוֹם at the end of the קַדִּישׁ and the עֲמִידָה, it is traditional to take three steps backward, then to bow to the left, to the right, and then forward. It is as if the person praying is leaving the presence of a king or a queen. Who is the Ruler whose presence we are leaving? _____

Answer the following questions in Hebrew:

1. In עֹשֶׂה שָׁלוֹם, what do we ask God for? _____

2. For whom do we want peace? _____

Copyright © 2004 by Behrman House, Inc; Millburn, NJ. www.behrmanhouse.com; Author: Terry Kaye; Contributing Authors: Claudia Grossman and Lori Justice; Artist: Ilene Winn-Lederer; Photographs: Terry Kaye (2), Gila Gevirtz (5); ISBN 978-0-87441-769-2 (Kaddish); Manufactured in the United States of America.

ISBN 978-0-87441-769-2

9 780874 417692 >